CONTENTS

FORWARD

BY

AMANDLA B. WILLIAMS

There once was a time where love and respect was the way of life for our people. Even though dishonor, hatred, and crime have replaced the love and respect throughout this community, "Let the Truth be Told" is the beginning to retrieving the love, sincerity and peace we once had. Mr. Dave Queeley's work not only gives hope to the younger generation, who have been lead astray from reality by Satan's evil doings, but also to the older generations, who remembers how it was to live peacefully.

A community without morals and values cannot sustain itself. Throughout this book you will find Mr. Queeley's understanding of how serving love, justice and good intentions can make, not only oneself stronger, but also a community becomes so unified that they can fight off evil and any other bad intentions together.

With all these senseless crimes and killings, crime makers must realize that they are not only committing crimes against each other, but themselves. Mr. Queeley's work is the start of letting these crime makers realize they are committing a form of genocide against themselves, each other, and future generations.

The youths of today are the ones to take care of us tomorrow. What will happen if they are not raised properly? Will the cycle of the older generations teaching the younger generation cease to exist altogether? "Let the Truth be Told" shows that black families are close knitted and that the cycle mustn't be broken. The family is the foundation of a COMMUNITY.

The people must have something to believe in. The Creator of All Things must be present in the lives of all today. Without the Creator all the pain and suffering will continue to exist. Mr. Queeley's book allows the readers to see the connection of how serving love, justice, and good intentions and believing praising the Creator will bring back peace and sincerity.

IT'S TIME FOR A CHANGE, SO LET THE TRUTH BE TOLD!!!

14 INCHES

By
Dave R. Queeley

From the fields of blood and blasphemy or from the rising of the sun or until the setting of the moon **14 INCHES** is the beginning of serving love, justice and good intentions. It's **14 INCHES** from the head to the heart.

If you don't have love in your head, it will never be in your heart. If a truth seeker have hate or prejudice in his/her heart they are spiritually and mentally committing murder against **14 INCHES**.

There is no limitation to what **14 INCHES** can truly accomplish if truth seekers only let the Creator in their life for real 7 days a week, 24 hours a day, because the Creator is good all the time.

If a truth seeker's heart is not right with love, justice, and good intentions there isn't no telling what they will do for the love of money, sinful ways, or disrespect.

I AM MR REALISTIC.

REALISTIC means true to life or nature, having or showing an inclination to face facts and to deal with them sensibly, some people now living have forgotten that the heart beats everyday saying, **"DO GOOD, DO GOOD, DO GOOD."**

They are not listening to **14 INCHES** not even for one minute.

The time has come for no more misrepresentation of the truth. It is time to listen to **14 INCHES** all the time. It's the right thing to do in life with confidence, dignity and pride.

Be true to the mission of **"GOOD WILL CONQUER EVIL AND LOVE WILL TRIUMPH OVER HATE."**

14 INCHES

MR. REALISTIC II
WANTED DEAD OR ALIVE
By
Dave R. Queeley

Hello World, I know my life will be in danger for telling the truth and for spreading the Creator's original plan of GOOD WILL CONQUER EVIL AND LOVE WILL TRIUMPH OVER HATE. If I must die for our communities, neighborhoods and all young people to sight up the Creator. SO BE IT!

Actions speak louder than words. I came not as a lamb to be murdered, but as a lion to rise in truth, love, justice and always, good intentions. I will never be afraid of disrespect or the dark side because the Creator said, "Let there be light and love so mankind don't have to continue to live in spiritual and mental darkness. The light is always serving honor, loyalty and having respect.

Mr. Realistic will be the new bridge builder; building bridges back to having respect or returning to love, justice and good intentions as the number one priority of our communities, neighborhoods and all young people.

Mr. Realistic was once a bonifide gangster, but now he's a soldier of righteousness on the battlefield who will be wanted dead or alive in the future by the system. Mr. Realistic's point of view will be to favor or sponsor ideas that make sense and to challenge our communities, neighborhoods and all young people to rethink the customary ways of doing the Creator's business or original plan. Realistic will never be afraid to talk about anything or say whatever is on his mind. It's time to take a stand against evil, sinful ways and disrespect.

Mr. Realistic will be the C.E.O. of the Common Sense Movement that will be about all people (black /white) uniting and moving love, justice and good intentions to a whole other level of having respect. If there is going to be any positive change, it has to come from everyone not just a privileged few, but from everyone living in Creation.

They have to remember disrespect and violent behavior are an abomination to our communities, neighborhoods and all young people's future of continuing the Creator's original plan of GOOD WILL CONQUER EVIL AND LOVE WILL TRIUMPH OVER HATE.

The Common Sense Movement will have the passion and leadership to find answers or real solutions to all the problems our communities, neighborhoods, and all young people now have to face in the 21st century.

Mr. Realistic will keep it gully enough to satisfy love, justice and good intentions so there will be no more mental and spiritual saloon gun fight or loss of life for no good reason at all. Realistic will be the new voice of example to all Colored Males in the 21st century who are now living like they are bullet proof that crime does not pay and to channel their anger into positive change and to teach them that their actions have serious consequences.

Mr. Realistic writings are informative and inspiring to touch as many hearts or lives to returning to having respect and serving love, justice and good intentions something the government or police cannot do which is to lift the spirit and to give hope.

MR. REALISTICE KEEPING IT REAL ALL THE TIME
AND
NEVER SCARED TO TELL THE TRUTH!
ONE LOVE, MR. REALISTIC

KEEPING IT REAL II

By
Dave R. Queeley

Samuel Blyden, this one for you, tell our boys stop the madness and KEEP IT REAL. As they live another day in the struggle of disrespect. KEEPING IT REAL is not a game and life is too short to be faking it until you make it.

In the 21st century the idea of KEEPING IT REAL or being real is somehow tied to going to jail, prison or getting shot and surviving is one of the worst myths in our communities and neighborhoods.

KEEPING IT REAL is standing strong for your family, communities and neighborhoods and to not let Satan's angels of destruction which is greed, jealousy, selfishness and disrespect continue to deceive young people into thinking evil is the boss. All the shootings and killings are proof that thugs on the corner need the Creator just as much as the disobedient believer.

KEEPING IT REAL is a very important message to getting the word out to all young people that the mission, battle or war must be continued 24 hours a day, 7 days a week, until GOOD CONQUERS EVIL AND LOVE TRIUMPHS OVER HATE.

KEEPING IT REAL will be a tool of economical and political empowerment and to increase the participation of all truth seekers to a worldwide call of action and not just lip service when it comes to finding true solutions to the problems that cause all the killings and shootings to continue to decimate our communities and neighborhoods. Truth seekers must canvas our communities and neighborhoods spreading the word or gospel that GOOD MUST CONQUER EVIL AND LOVE MUST TRIUMPH OVER HATE, and they must always remember NOT KEEPING IT REAL is spiritually, economically and mentally draining to our communities and neighborhoods. Serving love, justice and good intentions will not be based o politics or the ideology of evil.

It will be based on KEEPING IT REAL no matter how hard Satan's angel of destruction may try to tempt or deceive them into thinking he is the light of the world. Truth seekers must remember Satan's main job or priority is to destroy all traces of their past relationships, they had with serving love, justice and good intentions. Truth seekers keep doing real things and they are always on the grind spreading the word that GOOD MUST CONQUER EVIL AND LOVE MUST TRIUMPH OVER HATE.

KEEPING IT REAL is to bring life to the changing of values, conflicts and struggles that confront every truth seeker as they live their lives as an example of Creation's love. Our communities, neighborhoods and all young people need to be progressive not regressive when it comes to KEEPING IT REAL in the 21st century no more excuses. All young people must become the new extremist for love, justice and good intentions. RESPECT and KEEPING IT REAL with one another are the most important things our communities, neighborhoods, and young people need in their lives in the 21st century. When young people have respect for one another, KEEPING IT REAL or serving love, justice and good intentions will become easier.

If young people are going to KEEP IT REAL or be servers of love, justice and good intentions, our communities and neighborhoods needs better parental involvement in promoting or sponsoring the battle, war or mission of GOOD MUST CONQUER EVIL AND LOVE MUST TRIUMPH OVER HATE. In the 21st century some truth seekers have dreams of reviving love, justice and good intentions to the glory days of the past, where everyone KEEPS IT REAL with one another and they had respect for human life.

KEEPING IT REAL with one another will help in the fight against the enslavers, worshippers, traffickers of evil, sinful ways and disrespect. Throughout history KEEPING IT REAL and serving love, justice and good intention were truth seekers only survival tools for centuries. Truth seekers can't escape the consequences for letting Satan's angel of destruction continue to dictate how they now live in the 21st century. All truth seekers must remember that more than half of our government officials or law enforcement officers are now, "wolf in sheep's clothing" when it comes to KEEPING IT REAL or serving love, justice and good intentions, because when they get behind closed doors, no one knows what deals they are making with Satan's sinful ways or disrespect.

Our government officials or law enforcement officers continue to rob our communities, neighborhoods and young people of the chance to live in one love with respect because before they can become government officials or law enforcement officers they made too many promises or deals with Satan's sinful ways and disrespect to KEEP IT REAL in the 21st century. Truth seekers are tired of our elected government officials or law enforcement officers being so concerned about their image that they forget to tell the truth about who they're really working for is it evil or good. Some of them are now being influenced by Satan's angels of destruction or by his bribes of greed and they should be imprisoned for not KEEPING IT REAL or prompting love, justice and good intentions to the fullest in the 21st century.

KEEPING IT REAL and serving love, justice and good intentions will have the ability to change the consciousness or help young people stay alive and safe for the next five centuries.

KEEPING IT REAL DON'T DIE, IT MULTIPLIES.
ONE LOVE. KEEP IT REAL.

DRASTIC CHANGES

By

Dave R. Queeley

Free the mind and spirit from all propaganda

It's time for all believers to receive a stomach turning dose of reality. The time has come for some DRASTIC CHANGES in the way our communities, neighborhoods and young people serve love, justice, good intentions, and the Creator. All believers must always remember that the Creators original plan for love, justice, good intentions was opposed by the Angel whose name is Lucifer AKA Satan the Devil and he craves to be worshipped by mankind as the Messiah or Light of the World. The Bible does not contradict itself; believers are the ones who contradict the Bible by setting bad examples for non-believers to follow into the promise land of peace and joy. The Bible states that, "the son came to seek and save that which is lost." LUKE C19V10. There is nothing old fashion or out of date about teaching the Bible principles to non-believers or young people because the road connecting Satan the Devil and hell is getting busier and busier, while the road that connects the Creator and the words of wisdom, the traffic on that road has slowed down drastically, once in a while you will see a traveler on that road. Evil doers must abandon their wicked ways and stop being a slave to destructive thinking and Satan the Devil's vices and become a true worker or doer of THE CREATOR'S words of wisdom and love. In the bible at Luke C5V32 the son said, "I came not to call the righteous but the sinners to repentance."

It's time to shine a spotlight on disrespect, jealousy, selfishness and greed which are Satan's angels of destruction, because most believers have ignored them for far too long and it's hurting our communities and neighborhoods with robberies, murder, rape and drug dealing leading the way. It looks like believers do not care anymore if love conquer hate and will settle for anything. Believers have forgotten if you serve the Creator in truth what else do you need in life.

Our communities, neighborhoods and Christianity does not have the leaders who are willing to make the DRASTIC CHANGE from serving greed or Satan and who are really willing to going back to serving the Creator's love, justice and good intentions. They must remember that continuing to serve or sponsor evil, sinful ways or disrespect is like living under a dictatorship and that life is a roller coaster of suffering, pain and lots of nightmares. Some non-believers or young people are still waiting on the church, their communities and neighborhoods to change its way of doing the Creator's work that "Good will conquer evil and Love will triumph over hate." Believers can't rewrite the history of Satan's angels of destruction, but they can make history by going back to the Creator's words as a full time job. LOVE CAN'T LIVE WHERE THERE IS EVIL. It's like oil and water, they do not mix together. Believers should always remember there is no one immune to what's going on in the world; now movies, television and the inter-net has now become the new God.

Believers have been living in denial for years about the DRASTIC CHANGE that needs to take place in our communities and neighborhoods. Some believers are now doing an admirable job of trying to change or care for their communities and neighborhoods because they continue to encourage their children and other young people to apply the counsel of love, justice and serving good intentions to their lives so that the future of their communities and neighborhoods will be filled with peace and joy. Sadness, misery, and disrespect will be a thing of the past like the dinosaur. Serving love, justice, and good intentions are the Creator's greatest gift to all believers who continue to fight the battle of "Good will conquer evil and Love will triumph over hate."

Our communities and neighborhoods use to be stitched together by love, justice and good intentions, but now in the 21st century, they are now being held together by threads of greed, jealousy, disrespect, and most of all selfishness. Believers continue to fail to connect the dots of love, justice or good intentions and in the eyes of the Creator that's unacceptable behavior that cannot be tolerated any more. Believers continue to let themselves be conquered by evil, sinful ways and disrespect, that's the number one reason why they continue to lose the battle of good over evil. Our communities and neighborhoods continue to practice phoniness and hypocrisy when it comes to serving love, justice and good intentions because they continue to ignore the long and glorious history of the battle of "Good will conquer evil and Love will triumph over hate." True believers will never reign again as Kings or Queens if they continue to let evil, sinful ways and disrespect continue to decimate their communities and neighborhoods.

DRASTIC CHANGE will be the battle cry of any believer who is willing to pay the price to win the battle of "GOOD MUST CONQUER EVIL AND LOVE TRIUMPH OVER HATE." If all believers who know the Creator and love him with their mind, body and soul, "DEATH DOES NOT MEAN A THING."

DRASTIC CHANGE!!!

NO PANIC
By
Dave R. Queeley

Truth seekers will have no time to press the panic button because the revolution between good over evil will be seen on the television and heard on the radio for the whole world to see and hear what happened to hate and Satan the Devil. Truth seekers must always remember Satan the Devil is not patiently just waiting in Hell on non-truth seekers; he's all around as long as the spirit of greed, hate, jealousy, and selfishness continue to live freely. Some truth seekers continue to think mental and spiritual peace of mind is out of reach, which is a lie; because they should remember the Supreme Being is love not hate. The challenges ahead of truth seekers are enormous and the only way they are going to get through it, is together as one people serving good over evil and love must triumph over hate. Material things and evil continue to destroy the soul of our communities and neighborhoods. It's time to educate the public about the evils of disrespect and Satan the Devil and what hate is doing to our communities and neighborhoods.

The decision to start serving love, justice, and good intentions is both difficult and emotional, because truth seekers are fully aware of the impact of evil that has affected our communities and neighborhoods for too many centuries. The war overseas really makes the front page news these days, but the wars of evil over good continue to make the front page news, when another violent and senseless act is committed against our communities and neighborhoods. Truth seekers must not forget that the Creator's love does not include any political or negative things. It's something that is pure and clean. Truth seeker's primary goal now is not to panic, but to get back to the negotiating table of evil and work out a better deal for love, justice, and good intentions, because Satan the Devil and disrespect is running out of control with no end in sight.

The burden of reforming our communities and neighborhoods will take lots of time, hard work, and most of all communication and respect, because too many of our government officials and law enforcement officers have SOLD OUT to Satan's angels of destruction and have taken their bribe to continue to steal, conquer, and destroy in the name of love, justice, and good intentions. They must remember that serving love, justice and good intentions will have immediate results and change from Satan's world of ups and downs. Satan the Devil and disrespect is a restlessness that truth seekers can't seem to tame, but love is about educating people about the Supreme Being and raising the awareness level that "Good will conquer evil and Love will triumph over hate." After years of rising division, inequality and instability truth seekers must remember the government has a key role in making sure our families, communities, and neighborhoods have the right tools they need to succeed in life without stress from Satan the Devil and disrespect.

Justice, love and equality are just words in the dictionary that is not practiced in real life anymore. Truth seekers have forgotten about the spirit of love, justice and good intentions that kept them alive 500 years ago, during all of Satan's physical, mental, and spiritual experience of evil. It's important to share this information with as many believers as possible that there will be.....

NO TIME TO PANIC!

SPITFIRE

By

Dave R. Queeley

It's time for our communities, neighborhoods and young people to start spitting fire of love, justice and good intentions to burn down the angel whose name is Lucifer aka Satan the Devil, world of evil, sinful ways or disrespect that continue to run rampant in the 21st century, young people continue to lose their life and have no respect for the living. As the local reggae superstar Judah says, quote, "The parents keep complaining because the youths keep on dying, the government keeps on promising but they keep on stalling"

Our government officials or law enforcement officers are a bunch of heartless and gutless crooks that cannot stop the killings or shootings because they are involved in the sales of evil, sinful ways and disrespect to our communities and neighborhoods. Truth seekers must always remember they continue backsliding from serving or sponsoring love, justice and good intention because it does not make money like evil, sinful ways or disrespectful behavior. It's very important that our communities, neighborhoods and young people do not give up on the mission of "Good must conquer evil and Love must triumph over hate" until they find a reliable or satisfying answer or solutions to stopping all the killings, shootings, and disrespectful behavior.

In the 21st century our communities, neighborhoods and young people are now on the brink of self-destruction if all the killings, shootings and disrespectful behavior continues. It's time to take dramatic precautions to prevent this tragedy or disaster from happening. A lot of young people continue to glorify the wrong things in life, which is getting shot or going to jail or prison as a badge of honor and they keep on forgetting that serving or sponsoring love, justice and good intentions is a chance to prevent a future where every day young people lose their life to Satan's angels of destruction which are greed, jealousy, disrespect and selfishness.

SPITTING FIRE is just the beginning of a process to craft a binding pact to reduce evil sinful ways or disrespect in our communities and neighborhoods. It's very important to drive home the message that EVIL is temporary and LOVE is permanent. Our communities, neighborhoods, and young people continue to have no concrete, up front plan or commitment to returning to love, justice and good intentions. If they do not return to love, justice, and good intentions they are in danger of losing the most important battle or war in the 21st century, "Good will conquer evil and Love will triumph over hate."

Satan the Devil, evil and sinful ways knows truth seeker's greatest weakness is greed or selfishness, that's why his angels of destruction continues to infiltrate every aspect of truth seekers lives without a fight from righteousness. The split from Satan's evil or sinful ways will be very messy and gut wrenching for some truth seekers because they continue to be hearers of the words of the Creator, instead of doers of the words of the Creator. In the Bible aka the Good Book, it says at I John C4V8, "He who does not love, does not know the Creator, for the Creator is love."

Evil, sinful ways and disrespect continues to undermine truth seeker's moral defense that continue to result in spiritual disaster. All truth seekers must be willing to cut out of their lives anything that is spiritually harmful to the battle or war of "Good must conquer evil and Love must triumph over hate."

Remember,
LOVE IS NOT LOVE UNTIL YOU GIVE IT AWAY WITH A GOOD INTENTION. SPIT FIRE FOR REAL!!!

A RECIPE FOR DISASTER
By
Dave R. Queeley

Everyone by nature must engage in some sort of evil activity in this sick world, we now live in. Some people's actions can either blind us or liberate us from this material world, by performing actions for the pleasure of the Most High. Without selfish motives, one can become liberated from this mad society and attain knowledge of the self and Creation. Outward performance by all is needed to renounce the heart, mind and most of all the soul with the Creator, truth seekers will be purified by the fire of knowledge that will free the mind to eternal life.

Truth seekers need to start practicing to control their minds and senses and focus their time on the true holy land and mental unity. All who is manifested with this great mental power and by the fire of knowledge will see this holy land where the Creator said, "I go to prepare a place for you and where I go that you may go also." This place is for us to dwell forever in love and harmony. There is a battle under way for the soul of Christianity and it isn't a fight that soldiers of the war can win. This struggle put truth seekers (good) against non-truth seekers (bad).

Non-truth seekers have been fed a steady diet of lies and distortions about coming to church to serve the Creator. The Creator will hold truth seekers accountable for endorsing evil activities and living under false pretense. Truth seekers must save the church from becoming a way ward nation. The Devil has brought all mankind and Creation to the brink of destruction as a result of continuous evil activities and bad deals of the fake Christian people who are now running the church all over the world.

It's a conspiracy to destroy our knowledge of self, Creation and our glorious past as Creation's people. Truth seekers are allowing the conspirators to maintain their mental power and continue to control us spiritually with the root of Delilah, which is the root of deception. For our struggle is not against the flesh and blood but against the rules, against the authorities, against the powers of this dark world and against the spiritual forces of evil.

All the Devil's advice of influences has lead to the death of the body and the mind. The life of a truth seeker leads to everlasting life. Man is not in control, Creation is, brothers and sisters, know your place in the church. Darkness or evil can't watch the light or Creations words in the face and survive.

Prophecy must be fulfilled, the Creator said, "Heaven and earth will pass away before my words go void." Creation's love brings people together; it's the universal language of all truth seekers. Hate will no longer be a liability to truth seekers if they have faith in the Creator.

True Christian believers must always remember, "As it is in heaven, so it is on earth." Free the mind from all evil activities because that's the....

RECIPE FOR DISASTER.
IN CREATION NAME WE TRUST
NOT MAN

AMEN

TRAITORS
By
Dave R. Queeley

In the 1900's Loyalty, Respect, and Honor meant the world to our communities and neighborhoods. In the 21st century many government officials and law enforcement officers are traitors when it comes to serving love, justice, and good intentions, because their actions speak louder than words. They have misrepresented every step of serving love, justice, and good intentions and now they don't want the focus to be on them about how far Satan the Devil and Hate have deceived them into serving evil.

According to the dictionary, the meaning of a traitor is, "one who betrays another's trust; is false to an obligation or duty; one who commits treason."

Many government officials and law enforcement officers hate the light or serving love, justice, and good intentions because they want to live and sin in The Darkness, that's why they stay away from the light or serving love, justice, and good intentions for fear their actions will be exposed and they will be punished. Those who do what is right come to the light and serve love, justice and good intentions gladly do so. Everyone can see that they are doing what Creation wants them to do and that's serving love, justice, and good intentions with no misrepresentation of the truth.

One key principle of justice, love and serving good intentions is that a true leader must first get rid of the sinking ship mentality. A true leader does not hang back waiting to see what others are doing and then follow them. A leader for love, justice and good intentions is out front demonstrating how to live and act in the image of love. A true leader does not conform to the status quo but sets the standard for others to follow. A leader who follows the Creator's words of wisdom leads by example.

The murderers or extremist have moved to the increased use of indiscriminate shooting against our communities and neighborhoods with bullets without names and do not care who gets hit or killed. Truth seekers must remember all the shootings and killings are the side effects from a community and neighborhood being addicted to Satan the Devil and hate.

For century after century, decade after decade, year after year our government officials or law enforcement officers continue to give our communities and neighborhoods millions and millions of excuses why they can't find a solution to the problems that leads to all the shooting and killing. There is a lack of willingness to discuss why our communities and neighborhoods continue to be devoured by Satan the Devil and hate.

People are now scared to death to walk the streets of their communities and neighborhoods because of the fear of being raped, robbed, or murdered. The glow of the election and inaugural at the White House has faded so it's time for our government officials and law enforcement officers to start working on the change that the 44th president campaigned about, "Be the Change that you Seek."

Do your job! Our government officials and law enforcement officers must remember in Dr. Martin L. King's famous speech at the National Mall he said to a crowd of truth seekers, black and white who were truly serving love, justice and good intentions, "We must forever conduct our struggle on the high plane of dignity and discipline."

In the 21st century many of our government officials and law enforcement officers are now complete phony masquerading as servers of love, justice and good intentions while they continue to accept Satan's Bribes of Destruction. It's time for the spirit of Benedict Arnold to R.I.P.

WHO FEELS IT, KNOWS IT.
NO MORE TRAITORS

DENIAL
By
Dave R. Queeley

Truth seekers must realize how sad our situation would be without the powerful influence of love and the Creator's words of wisdom, they must never allow the preoccupation and anxieties of Satan the Devil and disrespect to continue to rob them of the opportunity to spread the good news that the Creator is love and "Love will triumph over hate and Good will conquer evil." It's time for truth seekers to stand on the shoulders of all those believers who came before them to spread and serve love, justice and good intentions without stress and fear from Satan the Devil and disrespect.

Truth seekers are still dealing with the residue effects of families torn apart in the cruel execution of physical and spiritual slavery and institutional racism that continues to keep truth seekers in denial about the effects of Satan the Devil and disrespect. Truth seekers are losing the battle of good over evil as a result of their own self inflicted mistakes, self-deception and self-delusion. Truth seekers must be willing to go the extra mile to make a contribution of love, justice and good intentions to their communities and neighborhoods that will last a lifetime. They must understand that serving love, justice and good intentions are a reflection of good spiritual training and responsible behavior.

Faithfulness, Righteousness, and Respect are three things truth seekers need in a large supply to win the war against Satan the Devil and disrespect. Satan the Devil and disrespect goes back for generations upon generations and truth seekers continue to let Satan make an evil world of greed, selfishness, jealousy and hate, that continues to be passed on to our future generation as the true way of life.

Evil is now paralyzing our communities and neighborhoods with help from murder, rape, and drug dealing leading the way. Satan the Devil and disrespect are now vulnerable and very paranoid about the fact that the Creator's love is about to conquer disrespect and evil in all dark places in our communities and neighborhoods and in the lives of all truth seekers. Time to stop dwelling on the past effects of Satan the Devil and disrespect and moving on to a future filled with honor, righteousness, and loyalty toward the Creator's words of wisdom.

Evil wins if Justice, Love, and Good Intentions continue to do nothing!

NO DENIAL!

THE STRUGGLE CONTINUES
By
Dave R. Queeley

Good will conquer Evil and Love will triumph over Hate.

Our communities, neighborhoods and Christianity are now being rocked by the perfect storm of unrighteousness. Some truth seekers continue to struggle with what is right or what is wrong while serving the Creator, love, justice and good intentions. There are many truth seekers who want to serve the Creator and give praise and there are some truth seekers who still want to serve what is wrong and that's living in darkness where Satan the Devil is the Messiah or Light of the world. Many Christian believers are in deep denial about what's right or what's wrong and have forgotten that Satan's sinful ways and disrespect is only a cheap duplicate of everything that is good and he will always be the leader to the false religion of what is wrong. All truth seekers are now called to become God's disciples of love in a godless era of Christianity where jealousy, greed, selfishness and disrespect are now running rampant.

Our communities and neighborhoods should never forget that all truth seekers and the Creator's greatest enemy is Satan the Devil and what is wrong living in darkness or sin. The Creator's final and greatest act in restoring Christianity was the blood of the son on the cross. All truth seekers should never forget that the Creator's love will shine through darkness and darkness can never extinguish it. Greed and Satan are not inseparable; you can't have one without the other because they are a package deal. Love, Justice and Good Intentions will be non-truth seekers LIFE RAFT after Satan leaves them out in the sea of darkness to be drowned by disrespect. Basically Satan is watching and waiting to see if truth seekers will sink or swim for the Creator, love, justice and good intentions. If they sink once, Satan will drown them with hate so it's better to swim to Holy Land or what is right.

Abandonment, anger, arrogance and betrayal are all words best used to describe Satan the Devil or what is wrong. Serenity, wisdom, harmony and faithfulness are all words used to describe the Creator or what is right, so why are non-truth seekers still struggling. The connection many truth seekers feel for Satan the Devil is far stronger than their sense of what is right. Their connection is that evil will conquer good and that's wrong. Truth seekers must be out of their minds if they think evil will ever conquer good. Heaven and Earth will crash before the Creator let that happen in this lifetime.

Nothing is too complicated that it cannot be simplified by the Creator's love and words of wisdom. All truth seekers must now evaluate everything in terms of whether it might be harmful or helpful to their effort of dealing with the crisis of disrespect, selfishness, jealousy and greed that truth seekers now have to face while serving love, justice, good intentions on their journey of "Good will conquer evil and Love will triumph over hate." The way truth seekers struggle to communicate with another about the Creator's words of wisdom and love makes it look bad in the public's eyes because non-truth seekers continue to see disrespect, selfishness, jealousy, and greed living free and happy in church without a notice of eviction from truth seekers.

Christianity now needs a church stacked to the rafters with truth seekers who are trained to know "Good will conquer evil and Love will triumph over hate" and are ready and willing to spread the good news. Like the Bible scripture that mentions that all truth seekers must "Go into the world and preach the gospel to every creature," Mark C16V15. Truth seekers must realize that disrespect, selfishness, jealousy, and greed is changing the world of Christianity at a tremendous rate and truth seekers are sitting around doing nothing about the disaster that is about to happen.

Satan the Devil can't wait for this disaster to happen so he can continue to lead truth seekers astray from the Creator's words of wisdom and love, so he can finally conquer all the souls he needs to help him in his battle with good and love for the souls of Christianity.

The Bible and the Creator demands that all truth seekers strive to reach a deep spiritual maturity in the words of wisdom. It's a place where many truth seekers will never reach in life, if sinful ways continue to be their number one priority or if they continue to struggle with what's right or what's wrong. It's time for truth seekers to start appreciating and respecting all truth seekers from other religions because there is only one Supreme Being no matter what seekers may call him. If we confess our sins, he is faithful. All the chips of disrespect, selfishness, jealousy, and greed are stacked up against truth seekers if they continue to live a life full of contradiction and lies.

Satan the Devil will keep their backs up against the wall all the time, if they do not return to what serving love, justice, and good intentions was all about in the beginning. Each One: Teach One: One God, One Aim, One Destiny. No more struggling with what's right or what's wrong. May the Creator pour blessings into the lives of all truth seekers who struggle with what's wrong or what is right. Always remember.....

"THE CREATOR MAKES NO MISTAKE, SO STOP STRUGGLING."

TAKE CHARGE

By

Dave R. Queeley

Oppression shackles our vision while on our Christian journey of serving the Creator. All truth seekers must take aggressive measures to rebuilding the church, if we want to achieve mental harmony and spiritual unity. Five hundred years of mental and spiritual slavery has changed the course of church from being a place of love to a place of hate and greed.

We must shift gears and embrace a liberated life style that frees us from confused priorities and teach our dollar some sense by supporting Christian businesses and institutions. Too many Christians have been a minority for so long that they have absorbed that characterization into their personalities without recognizing it. It's time to change this mind state.

All Christian believers have a responsibility to spread the Gospel and wearing their wedding garment (Matthew 22) well and to always remember serving the Creator only gets better with time. All truth seekers need to start living a liberated life style and refuse to be quiet about the way hate is living in the church. Many Christian believers are still living outside the main stream of opportunity while in this dark world of greed. The task before truth seekers is to find ways to ensure prosperity for the masses and not for a privileged few.

Crime and hard drugs are tearing apart the inner fabric of our communities and churches. We are setting new records for crack and cocaine abuse and arrests, school dropouts and most of all re-drum, which is murder. Truth seekers, what's wrong with this problem? We need to do a better job of spreading the Gospel which is, Creation is love not hate. Let's set new records by uniting and continuing the fight for mental and spiritual unity from all evil spirits or activity.

Church, always remember the devil is just an illusion. It's time to take charge of our destiny and seek love.
AMEN

HATE PROOF
By
Dave R. Queeley

Time to Hate Proof church with love, no more dark nights or days for the soul of Christianity. Love, justice, and serving good intentions are keys to Christian's unity and peace of mind, not hate.

Christian haters keep on talking about love and justice but still don't want to face the truth and facts that hate is crippling the church from serving the Creator in truth and righteousness.

It is time Christians start setting better examples in the name of Creation and stop contradicting the Words of the Creator. The Devil continues to feed truth seekers with thoughts of selfishness and greed, as Satan continues to dictate the future of church.

It is time for church to cleanse its consciousness of all evil spirits and activities that continue to live in the house of the Creator daily. Church needs a new approach to winning back justice, love and good intentions; this approach involves shifting the focus of church away from hate, greed, disrespect and destruction.

It is time truth seekers start operating by faith and love based on what the Creator's words have said in the Bible, instead of operating by hate, greed, and destruction based on what the dark world of the Devil has to say.

Many Christians are spiritual prisoners of greed and selfishness and remain locked behind bars of unrighteousness and bound by shackles of jealousy and sin. With true love, church will leave Satan the old dragon totally defeated and no more evil spirit or activity will ever control church and its people again.

Church must rely on the truthfulness of the Creators love and Words of Wisdom; time to get Satan the Devil's unbelief out of church, without faith it is impossible to love the Creator. Love and faith is something to share, it is not a treasure Christians keep for themselves, and it belongs to all truth seekers.

Christians must know if you were raised within Creation, without faith, it is impossible to please the Creator. The gospel of the Creator has stood by truth seekers for hundreds of years. It is not acceptable behavior to let our brothers and sisters down who continue to serve the Creator in truth and right. Always remember the number one commandment is, "HAVE NO OTHER GOD BEFORE ME."

Church will face a maximum sentence of death with no negotiation or plea agreements and no chance of parole if it continues to lead truth seekers astray from the Word of the Creator which is, CREATION IS LOVE NOT HATE.

Loving the Creator is not always rewarded with love, but sometimes with hate and jealousy. John Chapter 8 Verse 12, the Son said, "I AM THE LIGHT OF THE WORLD WHOEVER FOLLOWS ME WILL NEVER WALK IN DARKNESS BUT WILL HAVE THE LIGHT OF LIFE." Serve love not hate and stop living in spiritual darkness the only power that hate has is what truth seekers give it.

P.S. Before I leave I want to share a chapter with you that can make a difference in your life. If you are a true Christian believer, James Chapter 5 Verses 16-20.

TIME TO STOP HATING.

TRUE BELIEVERS
By
Dave R. Queeley

Anyone who believes will not believe over night, it takes time. If you keep trying you will get it right. At one point in time we all served sin, but that service only brought death to the body. Now our service is to a new master who provides righteousness and holiness that leads to eternal life. As true Christians believe we must allow the Holy Spirit to bring our living condition up to our legal position in this new life. Everything must change and the right way of living comes only through the union with Creation. When the Creator is ready to cash in these physical chips, I don't think Christians are ready to face this eternal fire that is coming our way very soon. We can't afford to go through this after all we've been through in this dark world for the last 500 years, so the only thing for us to do as a Christian family for the next 500 years is to seek the Creator.

All truth seekers are sick of chasing this runaway freight, which is the love of money; it's the root of all evils. "Seek ye first the kingdom of God and all these things shall be added on," we don't need a million dollars to seek the Creator because the, "meek shall inherit this earth," to me this means all the poor folks with the Creator shall have all the money and vanity and will have ever lasting life.

When your brains have been lift from the veils of the dark world, there's only one thing left to worship, the Creator. Church has become no more than a social club for truth seekers instead of a place to come and worship the Creator in truth and love. It's time true Christian believers stop complaining, criticizing, or gossiping while inside the church, to hear the words of the Creator, which is love. Truth seekers must stop calling non-truth seekers a bunch of out casts or misfits and start doing something good to bring them back into church. Non-Christians must be the stones that the church uses to continue building the bridge back to the Creator's love. The church is the Creator's masterpiece of love; it teaches us how to love the Creator and each other. Christians have a responsibility to tell non-truth seekers about the Creator's glory and love.

2 Corinthians 5:17 should be the motto of all truth seekers," therefore if any man be in Christ, he is a new creature, old things have passed away be hold all things become new." Ask not what church can do for you, but what true Christian believers can do for the church. The gates of hell shall not prevail against truth seekers. Church has lost its power to be a leader to non-truth seekers. If church can't satisfy the spirit how can church satisfy the physical. It's time church stop playing mind games with itself.

It's time truth seekers open the doors of their hearts to non-truth seekers because people don't last forever, the only thing that lasts forever is the Creators love.

SEEK CREATION NOT HATE

TRUE BELIEVERS II
JUST CHURCH GOERS
By
Dave R. Queeley

So many truth seekers have gone to church as kids and when they become adults, if asked what you call yourself they will always say "I'm a Christian" instead of just saying "I'm a church goer", because they still don't have a real understanding of what the Creator's original plan and Laws of Life are all about. They spend more time on the negative side and less time on applying his plan and the Laws of Creation to their daily life.

The traditional interpretation of being called a Christian use to be focused on the relationship between the Creator, Creation and truth seeker. Now it's all about the money and power and a relationship with the Creator and Creation is nowhere to be seen. Truth seekers must stand undefiled from disrespect, dishonor and disunity and does not allow himself/herself to be corrupted by the sinful way of life and does not think, speak or do evil.

Church goers may only go to church on Sundays, but most weekends they really don't want to go because they would rather sleep off their hangover from partying on Friday and Saturday nights. They only wake up to go to church for the popularity contest and fashion show that's taking place on Sunday mornings. They are not there to hear the words of the Creator. They are only there to gossip about one another and to criticize what someone else is wearing.

Church goers are not doing what the Creator's original plan and the Laws of Creation calls for and now they have the audacity to stamp Christianity on the outside of this package of Satan's beliefs and practices, as godly. Truth seekers have forgotten that Satan is the father of all lies, murders and disrespect; he has continually and cleverly deceived church goers into becoming his servants of injustice.

There are some truth seekers who want love, justice and good intentions to grow and prosper, but Satan and his angels of destruction are not interested in that process happening. Love, justice and good intentions was once the world's first unified world religion and church, before it was infiltrated by Satan and his angels of destruction who now want their evil religion to always be number one on church goers mind.

Truth seekers cannot begin to grasp the enormity of the deception orchestrated by Satan and his angels of destruction to control the whole world because they continue to travel on the roads of disunity, selfishness and greed. Once truth seekers are organized with having respect, love, justice and good intentions it will be harder for Satan and his angels of destruction to infiltrate and cause disunity among them.

They must always remember Satan is the leader of the Gospel of Deception, Dishonor, and Disrespect. In the twenty first century he is now a messianic insurgent who believes his ideas, principles, and beliefs will conquer the world. Satan continues to motivate evil doers or non truth seekers into fighting against the return to having respect, love, justice and good intentions. He knows his wicked and sinful ways will finally be coming to an end. That's why evil doers and non truth seekers continue refusing to follow the mental and spiritual intent of the Creator's original plan and the Laws of Creation.

Satan knows people who are under his influence will find it easier to kill or tell a lie than to tell the truth or save a life. That's why they keep on rejecting the countless Bible scriptures teaching the need for OBEDIENCE AND LOYALTY to the Creator's Words of Wisdom and they have forgotten the Bible teaches that sin is a the transgression of the Laws of Creation and the Creator's original plan. Truth seekers must never forget there are plenty of Bible scriptures that seek justice for the oppressed and for a world where the Holy One of love, justice and good intentions will reign forever.

Church goers now need to be taught there are no short cuts in achieving and living the Creator's original plan of good over evil and it will take hard work and relentless dedication to the core principles and values of love, justice and good intentions; only then, living for the Creator will happen and the top value will be nothing good comes easy and it does not happen fast, it takes time. Truth seekers have to make the strategic decision of returning to having respect, love, justice and good intentions because evil is running out of mental and spiritual steam.

When truth seekers return to having respect, love, justice and good intentions the great Creator of all Creation will begin to intervene directly and become more powerful than ever in their lives and there will be no more chains of injustice and planned doom.

Returning to love, justice and good intentions will be an indication that truth seekers and church goers are ready to be leaders in the cultural, mental and spiritual wars of good over evil and they will become stricter defenders of the Creator's original plan and the Laws of Creation. Returning to having respect, love, justice and good intentions will be the new revolution that won't be fought on the battle fields where blood and lives will be lost; it will be fought in the hearts and minds of people who are willing to see GOOD WIN THE SPIRITUAL AND MENTAL BATTLE WITH EVIL.

It does not take being a celebrity or having lots of money to make a difference, it only takes people who are willing to say the things that needs to be said and doing the things that need to be done. The Creator's original plan and the Laws of Creation are written in the hearts and minds of all that claim to be Christian, if they truly believe that the Creator is love. Church goers and truth seekers may come and go, but love, justice and good intentions ticks on forever.

Nothing can stop it!
TRUE BELIEVERS

TRUE BELIEVERS III
By
Dave R. Queeley

A true believer is an ambassador for love, justice and good intentions. They are always uplifting the Creator's original plan and following the Laws of Creation to the fullest on a daily basis. The Creator has made many promises in his words and each one has been or will be fulfilled. All truth seekers must observe the powers of injustice and planned doom in the world today and to never let evil spirits control them.

 Truth seekers must remember Creation is the canvas on which the Creator has painted the perfect picture that can never be duplicated. Truth seekers realize the Creator forgives all seekers iniquities and redeems their lives from mental and spiritual destruction. They understand knowing the Creator's original plan and the Laws of Creation will require a change of heart, mind and soul.

Love, justice and good intentions will cleanse all believers from all unrighteousness, injustice and planned doom that continue to run rampant and cause mental and spiritual problems to manifest in truth seekers lives. Satan and his angels of destruction will use every trick and resource available to him to help him in the battle of good over evil. Nothing will keep good from fiercely attacking him and conquering evil once and for all to never resurface. The Creator will deliver all truth seekers from the hands of our mental and spiritual enemies who want to see their death in the game of politics and power. A truth seeker must always be on guard not to misrepresent the Creators original plan and the Laws of Creation or let the delusions of their own mind continue to lead them astray from love, justice and good intentions.

Love, justice and good intentions use to be considered an essential ingredient of life, now it's a buried treasure that needs to be resurrected. The Creator will provide truth seekers with mental and spiritual protection and he will challenge them to suit up with armor. The mental and spiritual equipment are only effective when they are put on and used properly.

Our mental and spiritual stubbornness, stupidity and our willfully disrespecting and disobeying the Creators original plan and the Laws of Creation is now the problem. It's time for all truth seekers to start promoting unity and respect for the Creators original plan and the Laws of Creation to the fullest. The goal of a truth seeker is getting the gospel out or the good news that the Creator is love and not hate.

Only the Creator can make the mental and spiritual seeds of love, justice and good intentions grow, not Satan and his angels of destruction. They want to destroy these seeds which will grow into the tree of unity so they can become or be called god. No more misrepresenting the Creators original plan and the Laws of Creation. The Creator holds all truth seekers in his hands from the day we are born until we die. The Creator always cares and has love for them no matter what happens in their life. It's time to grow as an authentic truth seeker.

NO MORE WICKEDNESS AND SELF DESTRUCTION. TIME TO WAKE UP AND LIVE BECAUSE THE CREATOR IS LOVE NOT HATE

TRUE BELIEVERS RISE UP!

LIFE IN THE VIRGIN ISLANDS
By
Dave R. Queeley

When I was born, LIFE IN THE VIRGIN ISLANDS was truly a paradise where everyone lived in one love and unity. There was love, justice, and good intentions all around. Parents were real parents, children knew their place as children and the government was about doing the people's work that they were elected to do. A gun or a record setting murder year was something not heard of because life had value back then. Now in the 21st century LIFE IN THE VIRGIN ISLANDS has changed drastically.

There is no more love, honor and respect, only bloodshed or disrespect. Disrespect is the epicenter of the violence that continues to ruin LIFE IN THE VIRGIN ISLANDS that once was a paradise of love, justice, and good intentions. Now the fear of gun violence will soon drive many people to live behind gated walls with keypad entry systems, or with 24-hour video security system just to feel safe with LIFE IN THE VIRGIN ISLANDS.

It's going to take a much bigger mindset or focus to bringing back love, justice, and good intentions to LIFE IN THE VIRGIN ISLANDS. All Virgin Islanders must hold their heads up high because LIFE IN THE VIRGIN ISLANDS is now a very tough situation. If they continue to think about being defeated by disrespect or violence, then they shouldn't even be living IN THE VIRGIN ISLANDS with that mentality or attitude.

They've got to keep on fighting the battle of "Good will conquer evil and Love will triumph over hate," and stay together like Virgin Islanders of the past through thick and thin and to resist the temptation of Satan's angels of destruction. The expectations of Virgin Islanders are very high and although change always carries an element of risk of the unknown, there comes a time when that risk must be taken in an attempt to break through to new and higher levels of serving love, justice and good intention.

From sugar cane growers to beggar islands (tourism), that was the systematic plan that broke down the spirit of love, justice, and good intentions that kept them alive for centuries, now the results are a dog eat dog world or rat race, which now sees the dollar as God.

LIFE IN THE VIRGIN ISLANDS now has some Virgin Islanders scared to death to walk the streets of their communities and neighborhoods because of the fear of being raped, robbed, or murdered for no reason at all by disrespectful people. It is unacceptable behavior and defiance to the Creator's original plan that, "Good will conquer evil and Love will triumph over hate." It's time for all Virgin Islanders to take responsibility and help stop the spiral of violence and disrespect that continue to run rampant and trample on love, justice and good intentions.

 They must all look at the man or woman in the mirror because they all have done something that contributed to LIFE IN THE VIRGIN ISLANDS going down the drain. In the 21st century all Virgin Islanders must have the reputation as FIGHTERS OF DISRESPECT, VIOLENCE, and CORRUPTION. Some people still think the Virgin Islands is paradise but if they search deep, they will find Satan the Devil and disrespect is now the heart of paradise, not love, justice and good intentions.

Guns that are bought in the U.S.A. are causing the unnecessary killing and shooting in paradise. Some Virgin Islanders are still asking the question, "So how did they get here to cause so much trouble, war and bloodshed in the Virgin Islands." It's time all Virgin Islanders take a bold step to toppling disrespect and violence's choke-hold on LIFE IN THE VIRGIN ISLANDS and to start enforcing the rules of Creation which is serving love, justice, and good intentions like true Virgin Islanders of the past, who lived and died for freedom.

If Virgin Islanders continue to fall short of serving love, justice and good intentions there will be a dreadful price to pay, which is....

CREATION'S WRATH!

LIFE IN THE VIRGIN ISLANDS II

By

Dave R. Queeley

Life in the Virgin Islands is just another sad day in the book of injustice, misery and planned doom in what use to be called "America's Paradise". Life in the Virgin Islands now seems like the nightmare on Elms Street. It's time to begin the change and reform of turning the page in this book of injustice, misery and planned doom because "America's Paradise" has been stuck in a long evil rut of disrespect, dishonor and disunity for far too long. The returning to having respect, love, justice and good intentions which is long overdue will be the first step towards reversing the course of self destruction the Virgin Islands have been on for the last five decades.

Some Virgin Islanders now think in the twenty first century they have a rogue government system that is being operated by educated criminals and their team of goons who are called cronies. They are now operating like Modern Day Pirates who continue to plunder "America's Paradise for self gain or for their secret societies to make money which is the reason why life in the Virgin Islands is going down the drain fast with no end in sight. Virgin Islanders should not wait until something is affecting them for them to get up and get out and do something about this major problem.

It's time they renewed their vow from the past of non violence because life in the Virgin Islands is like a war zone, automatic gunfire night after night with no real end in sight. The reality is no one knows how many illegal weapons are out there in our communities and neighborhoods waiting and ready to cause havoc and always ready to take another life randomly, senselessly and unnecessarily for no good reason at all. Gun violence and crime continues to scare the hell out of some people. They would not even go outside in the day and going out at night time is out of the question, for fear of being robbed, raped or murdered.

We use to be a nation of diverse and positive people now we are a nation of diverse, greedy and selfish people. Virgin Islanders must remember if you live in a place you should have a say in the politics and government decisions because it's a freedom to be in charge of your own destiny and life. In the future a stream of light will pierce through injustice and darkness of ignorance until having respect, love, justice and good intentions enlightens the Virgin Islands about the Creator's original plan and the Laws of Creation. Life in the Virgin Islands is now a black hole of misery and Virgin Islanders suffering from mental, economical and spiritual pain every day. Improving the quality of live from second class citizenship to full citizenship will be the first step in stopping this oppression from continuing to happen in the twenty first century.

Life in the Virgin Islands has changed unexpectedly from "America's Paradise" of love them all, to the "America's Paradise" of kill them all. These actions continue to lead down the corridor of injustice and planned doom also known as DEATH ROW. Life in the Virgin Islands to some young people and children is now based on anything that is glittering. They do not savor life to the fullest any more. Life is now worthless to some of them. In the past five years, look how many young lives as the Gangster they would say GOT THROWN IN.

It's for real. Life to some young people isn't worth a penny and things are getting worse as the days pass by. Unsolved homicide cases are piling up in the Virgin Islands with no end in sight and the problem is "NO SNITCHING". So they will stay unsolved until someone has a change of heart and decides to tell the truth; so there will be an arrest in the case. Unsolved homicides have not sparked any public outcry and outrage over what many Virgin Islanders perceive as law enforcement ineffectiveness in the face of soaring gun violence and crime. They are simply incapable and lack the expertise and resources needed to solve cases. We have to realize that the police department do not have the means nor the skills to do an in depth investigation that will solve unsolved homicides. Unsolved homicides have plagued the Virgin Islands for several decades and they have added up to an outrageous number of lives lost.

Now in the twenty first century the body count of unsolved homicides still continue to grow. The low arrest rate has started a vicious cycle as witnesses hesitate to speak to police because they are too fearful of retribution from the enemy. We live on a relatively small island where everyone and the police were capable of solving crimes. Another big problem is the distrust that some Virgin Islanders have in the police department. A lot of times the witnesses to a violent crime does not want to speak out for fear of being murdered. That's one of the main reasons why life in the Virgin Islands is going down the drain from being "America's Paradise". Fake gang activity is now widespread in the Virgin Islands and it now fuels more than half of the criminal activities now taking place in our communities and neighborhoods.

All Virgin Islanders must never forget, a couple years ago the national drug intelligence center reported the U.S. Virgin Islands along with Puerto Rico are high intensity drugs and gun trafficking area, where guns are selling like hot cakes. Life in the Virgin Islands has now become the new Dodge City because it's not safe anymore, day or night you never know when you have to dodge bullets in broad daylight or become a victim of a violent crime.

Life in the Virgin Islands is not like by gone days when everyone had respect, love, justice and good intentions in their heart and on their mind. When it was the highest priority of life and the Creator's words, original plan and the Laws of Creation were followed to the fullest without any excuses. They knew the truth is like a ring, no beginning and no end. They never forgot their roots, staying undiluted and unedited. A single adjective is not sufficient to describing how bad life in the Virgin Islands has gotten from being called "America's Paradise.

All Virgin Islanders need to start standing up and crying out vociferously and in unison that they are not going to tolerate anymore flawed and BS ideas and policies from the people in charge because Life in the Virgin Islands has gone from bad to worse, the facts are evident. The overwhelming evidence against these people in charge leads to the conclusion that they only care about getting paid and cutting their deals in the darkness of injustice and planned doom. Visiting and living in the Virgin Islands is now a life threatening condition of injustice and planned doom. All Virgin Islanders should never forget their ancestors had principles, courage and unity to fight injustice and planned doom in high and low places so that Life in the Virgin Islands would improve and it would remain "America's Paradise" for future generations to come.

In the twenty first century those principles, courage and unity have died. Disrespect, dishonor, and disunity have taken over Life in the Virgin Islands. Solidarity is a word and something that is now impossible for Virgin Islanders to now accomplish. Gun violence and crime is one of many contributing factors to why Life in the Virgin Islands has gotten so bad from being "America's Paradise" and there are no preventive measures from stopping it from happening on a daily basis. It's time all Virgin Islanders wake up and join the team of good over evil.

Lately Life in the Virgin Islands is a constant struggle to stay alive and staying free from being a victim of a violent crime. Life in the Virgin Islands is not "America's Paradise" anymore.

STAY SAFE VIRGIN ISLANDERS

LIFE IN THE VIRGIN ISLANDS III
FROM BAD TO WORSE
By
Dave R. Queeley

Life in the Virgin Islands seems like it's going from bad to worse as the days go by. We the People are not standing up, fighting and speak out against what's now happening in the twenty first century. Bad policies and bad government are trying to enslave We the People back into the evil chains of poverty, misery and injustice. The disrespectful way the government of the Virgin Islands is now running is a travesty and insult to We the People's intelligence to live Life in the Virgin Islands, watching as it has gone from bad to worse.

We the People have to send a strong message to the people in charge, who are Sell-a-tors and Modern Day Pirates that we are not going to tolerate anymore government officials and workers who continue to steal and mismanage the people's money and future without due process of the law. There will be more pats on the back from Satan and his angels of destruction saying good job for your evil actions and attitudes. In the future there will be no more diplomatic immunity; it's now going to be go straight to jail or prison.

We the People cannot continue to keep on hiring or electing incompetent people to continue to manage the Virgin Islands into the ground and into non-existence. The Bureau of Corruption is what the Virgin Islands government system can now be called. The executive and legislative branches are now full of shit and out of touch with the people's needs for making Life in the Virgin Islands better lately. All they have done is continue to turn things from bad to worse. They offer no glimpse of hope and prosperity for the future of the Virgin Islands, so this will continue to make the Virgin

Islands a more dangerous place to live and visit. As the battle of change and reform Life in the Virgin Islands plays out.

Bad policies and bad government continues to shape and undermine its future. Bad policies and bad government will never take the true steps and actions necessary to saving the Virgin Islands from being destroyed by Satan and his angels of destruction who sees the Virgin Islands as one big piggy bank or A.T.M. machine.

The Virgin Islands Bureau of Corruption also known as the government system needs to pull itself back together and salvage the future of Life in the Virgin Islands, it is slowly going down the drain fast. The reason for Life in the Virgin Islands going down the drain is failure of management skills from top to bottom, incompetent performance on the job can be blamed too.

If something isn't done soon We the People can be prepared to face the possibility of the Virgin Islands filing for chapter 9 municipal bankruptcy protection. Bad policies and bad government continues to compromise the future and well being of the Virgin Islands with no end in sight. All the evidence that We the People have against the people in charge suggests that when the Circus comes back to town again also known as election time. It will be time to oust all incumbent from office and finally stop their misrule that has done nothing but help Life in the Virgin Islands go from bad to worse. They are now totally out of touch with the heart beat and pulse of the people who are suffering on a daily basis from electricity oppression, outrageous rent and mortgage payments and very expensive food and gas prices.

Some people now think the rapid rise in the cost of living that is sucking the blood and life out of them is because some of the people in charge who are members of Satan's secret society of injustice, destruction and planned doom. They want to see the

Virgin Islands as Anglo-Saxon as England is English. That's why they continue to let Life in the Virgin Islands go from bad to worse.

We the People have to go after everyone who is involved with the chains of injustice, destruction and planned doom the leaders, the suppliers, the brokers and the runners who continue to disrespect the native people. They have little or no appetite when it comes to doing what's right and positive for the people suffering. They continue to struggle to find solutions to all the social ills we now face and to halt and crack down on bad policies and bad government tight grip on power.

We the People cannot and should not remain silent about the fact that the Virgin Islands going down the drain fast because of bad policies and bad government. Bad policies and bad government is full and unimaginable and it's now a public spectacle that will not bridge the gap between the haves and the have not's. We the People should have one thing in common and that's to fight for the independence for bad policies and bad government. Satan the Devil also known as the angel named Lucifer has brainwashed and paid off politicians and high ranking government officials.

They are the ones who are suppose to make the people's lives better. But on the other hand, they are the ones who are making all the bad decisions that have changed Life in the Virgin Islands from bad to worse. Virgin Islanders cannot continue reading the newspaper and seeing articles about their government system bad behavior or turning on the radio and television and hearing about these evil actions without getting furious about how far down the ladder and drain Life in the Virgin Islands has gone.

All Virgin Islanders will be held accountable by the Creator for letting life get so damn bad and for letting politicians and high ranking government officials run amuck and we stand by and continue to do nothing to stop them or to get them fired. Bad policies and bad government continues to assure the people that

Life in the Virgin Islands is going nowhere because it was designed specifically for the people to fail, never to see prosperity anytime soon. Bad policies and bad government has been well documented in the Virgin Islands. In the twenty first century politicians and high ranking government officials are now preaching the same words as gangster rappers," get rich or die trying". Life in the Virgin Islands has gone from bad to worse. As the saying goes from the Wizard of Oz,"There is no place like home."

THE VIRGIN ISLANDS.

DYING CHILDREN
By
Dave R. Queeley

In the 21st century, our children are now children of disrespect and are dying faster than soldiers of war. Life is too short and it's not a game so you better take advantage of it while you're young. Most people think only old folks die, but now in the 21st century children are dying faster than the old folks.

Parents need to start teaching their children how to live and act in the image of Creation, because their children's lives are full of injustice or sinful ways and is in need of a spiritual change of life. They must remember living for the Creator involves constant changing, learning, and growing in the name of love, justice and good intentions and to always remember the church is not just another building, but it's a holy place signifying the presence of the living Creator who is to be worshipped and praised 24 hours, 7 days a week.

As long as there are barriers blocking our children from serving the Creator, it will always look bad upon the church for not doing its job of saving lost souls. Writing our children off can never be acceptable behavior as truth seekers. The Commandments are the Creator's absolute rules for living for love, justice, and good intentions. No man has ever perfectly kept all of the Creators laws except for the first born of Creation.

The church that continues to sow injustice, destruction, and evil will harvest disaster and death. It's time to bring real love, justice, and serving good intentions back to our communities, neighborhoods, and church and truth seekers must never forget that the Creator is love and not hate. Parents must join together in an effort to change attitudes, feelings and behaviors regarding coming to church to serve the Creator in truth and honor. They can no longer ignore what hopelessness, hate and disrespect are doing to their children by continuing to send them to an early grave.

In the Bible it is said, "If you have faith the size of a mustard seed nothing will be impossible for you." Matthew C17V20. Parents must realize if they are true believers in the Creators words of wisdom, they must teach their children the love, understanding, and compassion that the 1st son came and taught, love, justice and good intentions and to have respect for all mankind no matter the color of their skin, he was crucified for them to have everlasting life. Parents must come together to exhibit the love, compassion, and the understanding that We the People must always remember, "IT TAKES A VILLAGE TO RAISE A CHILD."

Remember the love of a village continues to die in our communities and neighborhoods, while selfishness, greed, and disrespect continue to be on a rampage. Our children need encouragement to forget about the neglect, abuse, and violence they have to live through in this dark world of evil and sin.

In the 21st century, no one is trying to teach our children how to live or act in the image of Creation. The Creator is love that has NO LIMITATIONS. Without children the future of our communities and neighborhoods is PITCH BLACK. It's time to PUT UP or SHUT UP and save our children from dying.

STAY ALIVE CHILDREN, STAY ALIVE!!

DYING CHILDREN II
Stop watching TELL-LIE-VISION
By
Dave R. Queeley

In the 21st century, respect and serving love, justice and good intention must become our dying children's new moral guide out of the fields of violence and the streets of disrespect and to continuing the battle of "Good will conquer evil and Love will triumph over hate." Parents must find a way to ease the pain of why their children keep on dying young. They must stop throwing love, justice and good intention up in the air or against the wall of hate and start serving or returning to it.

Parents must remember parenting was the first profession of the world, now it has been devalued to nothing but a word in the dictionary. It's time to shift from silence and denial about the calls to face the enemies from within who continue to wreak havoc on our communities, neighborhoods and schools and it's called friendly fire. Parents our children are now being called Generation X and they continue reaping the rewards of Satan's angels of destruction, which is death or life in prison; and no one is doing nothing to stop the slaughter of our children of this win-less war, like Vietnam.

Parents want to see actions not just rhetoric or lip service from their so-called government leaders and they want the police to stop just patrolling and start really protecting and serving. And remember any individual who breaks the law and commits a violent crime with a gun should be brought to justice and face stiff penalties for their actions not be rewarded with a slap on the hand or pat on the back any more. In the 21st century it is certain that a better prevention plan should have been in place decades ago and maybe it would have prevented the recording setting 51 deaths in one year.

"SEEK THE WORLD AND LOSE YOUR SOUL OR LIFE," is now our children's motto or number one priority in the 21st century. Parents must teach their children to forget about the cash, chains and fancy cars with big rims because they are physically rich, but they are still broke and poor in the spiritual and the mental when it comes to the Creator's original plan of love, justice and good intentions; because there is no discipline, honor, and loyalty which is essential for them to be successful in the battle of good over evil. Without a change in behavior, it will be very difficult or if not impossible for love, justice and good intentions to make any progress against Satan's angels of destruction.

LACK OF ADEQUATE EDUCATION, LACK OF POSITIVE PARENTING, LACK OF ECONOMIC OPPORTUNITY, LACK OF RESPECT, HONOR, and LOYALTY are some of the reasons why our children continue to relocate to the cemetery or life in prison. There is no opportunity for our children to grow and excel in the battle of "Good will conquer evil and Love will triumph over hate."

Negative influences continue to run rampant, taking our children's lives along the way. So, it's time to get parents more involved in promoting or sponsoring love, justice and good intention. It's the first step for positive influences to take back over our communities, neighborhoods and schools. Parents must continue fighting in the memory of respect to regain control of their homes, dwellings and schools and they must never forget that prophecies from the book of Revelations are being revealed every day: CHILDREN HAVING CHILDREN and CHILDREN KILLING CHILDREN (or PARENTS).

STOP THE CHAOS AND CONFUSION DYING CHILDREN

COLORED MALES

By

Dave R. Queeley

"IDOL MINDS AND HEARTS ARE THE DEVIL'S WORKSHOP."

In the 21st century Colored Males are fueled by the spirits of hate, greed, jealousy and selfishness and have forgotten that love, justice and serving good intentions are the key to longevity. It's time Colored Males dig themselves out of the hole of evil they've been living in for the past 500 years. For the Colored Male to survive another 500 years, they will have to forget about Hollywood and serving Satan the Devil and to look for something that is far greater than them, which is the Creator, who has control over life and death, no matter what you may call him. Remember the goal of longevity must be accomplished if Colored Males are going to survive another 500 years. Colored Males must never forget there are no shortcuts in life.

If they start searching the scriptures of the Bible AKA the Good Book they will make amazing discoveries concerning the love of the Creators and the words of wisdom. The Creators love and words of wisdom are something so precious and so rare it cannot be denied. The success of being a Colored Male is first to have a love for the Creator and words of wisdom and secondly, to treat one another as you want to be treated, with love and respect and not hate. Most Colored Males see success as the accumulation of material bondage without debt, owning a house, driving an expensive car or being able to walk into a store and buy anything they want, but they keep on forgetting who woke them up in the morning, it was not Satan the Devil, it was the Creator. Colored Males must always remember the Creator is not just for the famous and rich or those people who dress up to go to church like it's a fashion show and have forgotten that the supreme gift of love is for everyone to share in the name of Creation.

"Seek his will in all you do and he will direct your paths," Proverb C3V6. Some Colored Males have tried Satan the Devil's way of life and found it to be an empty way of life. Serving Satan the Devil will turn into a long nightmare of evil ups and downs if they continue to live like they have all the time in the world to serve love, justice and good intentions. Since the beginning of time of man, Colored Males have been on the merry go round of evil and greed and they are still slaves to negative thinking and to a negative life style where Satan the Devil has all the power and he is worshipped as the Messiah. Most Colored Males are still stuck on stupid. It's been called the crab in the barrel syndrome, the animalistic instinct that makes them want to pull the trigger on a brother or sister just as he or she is about to claw their way out of the barrel of hate and greed and into a better way of life which is serving love, justice, and good intentions and not hate. The Creator's words of wisdom and love must now keep the peace when," STOP SNITCHING!" is now the battle cry for some Colored Males.

The Colored Male must now teach and lead by example on how to live with moral courage and to make clear and good decisions for the next generation to follow into eternal life not eternal death; they need to learn patience and the value of unselfish love. Unselfish love is when you are NOT looking for something in return when you have done a good deed. It's time to challenge the government that has been historically unjust to the Colored Male not needing attention or totally out of reach and not worth the effort or expense of trying to save the Colored Male is the attitudes of our fake leaders who are elected to represent us.

Society and the government has no excuses for not realizing that all the murders and rapes are not going to fix the mental or economical problems that the Colored Male now has to face to survive in this sinful world we now live in. The injustice perpetrated against the Colored Male can be seen on television, you can read it in the newspaper or a magazine, and you can hear about it on the radio, another Colored Male died from another gunshot. Serving love, justice, good intentions and the Creator's words of wisdom are the ultimate answer to all of the Colored Males problems in life. Some true believers are convinced Colored Males are their own worst enemy and they are truly heading for self destruction, their values on life have gotten worse.

All the Colored Male now cares about are fancy cars with big rims, selling drugs and killing their own people for the love of money. Violence is something Colored Males deals with every day while living in the ghettos of hate and greed, but after all the funerals and crying is over, it's right back to killing each other and serving Satan the Devil. Most Colored Males only think of the blood shedding only when they are the victims of a hate crime. The homicide rate among Colored and Latino Males are out of control.

If this continues to happen they will become an endangered species or like the dinosaur, a thing of the past. Society and the government must always remember the victims and perpetrators of gun violence are getting younger and younger and it's sad to see the prison population is getting younger and younger, too. It's like we're living back in the wild, Wild West days when human life did not mean anything, only the bullet ruled not love or justice.

IN THE NAME OF THE CREATOR
STOP THE BLEEDING

COLORED MALES II
By
Dave R. Queeley

Mr. Realistic is a gorilla reporter AKA CNN of Love reporting from the highways, byways or the trenches of evil, the ghettos, which are now called our communities and neighborhoods. All believers must remember the struggles or problems of the Colored Male takes no time off or vacation. Colored Males are now living in a world where no one is really free from economical, mental or spiritual slavery. It's time for a new beginning against the oppressiveness of Satan the Devil and hate. When people are organized they can always change laws and make a better system, for better living conditions for all believers to live without stress and fear of Satan the Devil and evil.

Colored Males are now mental, economical and spiritual slaves to Satan's society of evil and they continue to build his empires of hate up to destroy them daily. It's time believers use their dollar wisely and build their own communities and neighborhoods of love to help in the fight against mental, economical and spiritual slavery that continue to grow and live in the ghettos of greed and selfishness. Remember greed, selfishness and disrespect offer nothing to our communities and neighborhoods but misery and death. Serving love, justice and good intentions will bring prosperity and peace. Believers must never forget about the Devils that ruled our communities and neighborhoods for 500 years of free labor.

Crimes of mental, economical, and spiritual slavery cannot be forgotten or forgiven. Believers must pressure Satan the Devil until he gives back our communities and neighborhoods to love, justice and serving good intentions. The spirit of evil should not continue to dictate how the Colored Male now lives in the 21st century, because serving evil, sinful ways or disrespect have unpredictable side effects that no good doctor can cure. Believers must always remember Satan the Devil and hate use to lynch the Colored Male at night time but today in the 21st century as the world turns, they now do it to themselves in the BROAD DAY LIGHT for everyone to see, good and evil people. The Colored Male cannot solve the problems of Satan's sinful ways and disrespect on their own and the world cannot solve them without the Creator's love and words of wisdom.

One voice of love may go unheard, but the voices of many will have such a resounding effect that the Creator's love and words cannot be ignored anymore. Colored Males must always remember the story of serving Satan the Devil and evil are a story of colossal failure and a death sentence of eternal hell fire. Serving Satan is like living in a chicken cage because going to prison or jail is a living hell. Satan, disrespect and sinful ways have robbed many Colored Males of their character, respect, and life. In the 21st century they must try to maintain and not lose sight of their commitment to the Creator's love and words of wisdom because knowing the truth shall set them free from evil, sinful ways and disrespect.

The Colored Male now has a duty of being a light of love, justice and good intentions in all the dark, evil places on earth and they must advance towards a society where disrespect, poverty, violent crimes and ignorance are all diminished. In the 21st century solving the mental, economical and spiritual crisis in the Colored Males' homes or lives could be the keys to stopping all the shootings, killings and conflict that continue to destroy our communities and neighborhoods. The sooner our communities and neighborhoods take affirmative action to reviving love, justice and serving good intentions, the sooner our communities and neighborhoods will see a true change or cease fire!

Mr. Realistic AKA CNN OF LOVE, do not want to sound racist, but I am only stating a true fact, "All the people who own the manufacturing companies that make the guns and bullets of evil are not people of color. All the people who transport the guns and bullets of evil on their yachts, private airplanes or jets are not people of color." So if all believers want the gun problem to stop in their communities and neighborhoods, they need to go to the top and STOP MARCHING AND WALKING at the bottom that only continues to achieve nothing because the killings and shootings still continue to destroy the Colored Males lives. Remember the manufacturing companies are the problem and it's called Supply and Demand. The Colored Males must learn the rules of serving love, justice and good intentions or the codes of life, if they want to survive for another 500 years and they must remember that the Creator is love and death to evil or sinful ways.

The more light our communities and neighborhoods shine on evil, sinful ways and disrespect the safer the Colored Male will be in the 21st century!

COLORED MALES STAY POSITIVE!

COLORED MALES III
BARAK H. OBAMA
By
Dave R. Queeley

It was B.C. before Christ and A.D. after the death. Now in the 21st century it's B.B. before Barak and A.D. after Barak. President Barack Obama's inauguration on January 20, 2009 as the 44th President of the United States of America will represent one of the most significant events in history, not only Black or American, but world history. President Barack Obama is now a mighty tool in the hands of the Creator. It is very important to remember that President Barack Obama is not the messiah for race relations in this country, but just another Colored Male doing his part in the battle of, "Good must conquer evil and love must triumph over hate." The 13th Amendment abolished slavery but segregation ran rampant for 500 years. Blacks were given the right to vote in 1965, but it took 43 years for an African American to rise to the nation's highest office.

Martin Luther King Jr. gave his life to break down the barriers of hate in our society's struggle for equality. Believers must never forget he also gave his life fighting to give everyone a chance to realize his dream that, "Good must conquer evil and love must triumph over hate." Believers who are willing to move on to spiritual love and serving good are willing to pay any price for the Creator's love. These are the people who the Creator uses in special ways to shape the world. President Barak is a perfect example of where serving love justice and good can take you in life.

Serving love, justice, and good intentions offers a blue print for overcoming Satan the Devil and his angels of destruction which are greed, jealousy, hate and most of all selfishness. Colored Males must remember serving love, justice, and good intentions is a journey where at the end, there will be streets paved with gold, but serving Satan the Devil and hate is a journey where there will always be ups and downs and the end result will b e total destruction or death. Love must become a lightening rod of lasting change in our communities and neighborhoods and in the lives of all believers who believe in the Creator's words of wisdom.

Racism will always be evident in the way Colored Males are treated by the police, the courts and never forget about the correction systems, a modern day concentration camp that is a living hell 365 days a year. Colored Males must never forget about the horrors of the middle passage, when their ancestors were packed into the hulls of slave ships on their way to America AKA the New World. Colored Males must always remember they are the offspring of those people who suffered and died on that horrible journey of hate so they must never forget them spiritually or mentally.

No more excuses, we can't blame the MAN anymore, all of that changed when Obama was elected to the White House. President Barak Obama's election and inauguration will always represent from the slave ship to the White House. In the 21st century Colored Males must find a way to live harmoniously as equals and everyone must choose love and unity over fear, separation or death. Martin Luther King Jr. final dream will not be complete until disparities in health care, education, and economics are totally eliminated.

President Barak Obama's election on November 4, 2008 says to every Colored Male that their dignity and destiny are now in their own hands and they can now become anything they dream of being in life, even the President of U.S.A. It's time for the Colored Male to pull themselves out of the dark abyss of hate and grief and move on to a better place where love, faithfulness, and loyalty rules. Before the Black Panther, Martin Luther King Jr. and now President Barak H. Obama there was the great Marcus Garvey, the Prophet. Obama's success was made possible by the strong foundation laid by Marcus Garvey decades ago. All believers must never forget when you celebrate Obama; you celebrate all who died in the struggle and fight against Satan the Devil and hate. From the north to the south, east to west, from African to the Caribbean, believers have invested their faith, love and hope in President Barak Obama and are now waiting to see if a change is really going to come. Believers are not celebrating Barak Obama; they are celebrating America finally trying to live up to its creed that all men are created equal.

COLORED MALES IV

IT'S A BLOOD BATH

By

Dave Queeley

Don't believe the hype that Colored Males have reached the mountaintop that Dr. Martin Luther King Jr. once talked about just because Barack H. Obama, a Colored Male (50%) is in the White House. Believers must put things in perspective that Satan the Devil and hate still has the Colored Male on a wild goose chase.

 It's a BLOOD BATH everyday of the week and Satan the Devil and hate continue to deliver their version of the Iraq war on the streets of our communities and neighborhoods. Every day in our communities and neighborhoods should be called "MEMORIAL DAY" because so many Colored Males continue to lose their lives carelessly with help from the Great Deceiver named Satan, who continues to turn our communities and neighborhoods into cemeteries.

Colored Males have to start taking responsibility for their actions of letting Peace and Justice continue to go down the drain and must always remember, serving love, justice and good intentions need dedicated individuals who will share a common mission to fight evil in all dark places and to contribute to our communities and neighborhoods a positive image of peace and justice and to make them a safer place to live without stress and fear of Satan the Devil and hate.

In the 21st century Satan the Devil and hate is either directly or indirectly involved in the violence, mental wars, and misery that afflict the Colored Males. It's Satan the Devil and disrespect and our government officials who are to be blamed for the Colored Males world of suffering not the Creator's words of wisdom or serving love, justice, and good intentions. In the Bible AKA The

Good Book, there is a scripture that says, "Without faith no one can please the father, anyone who comes to the father must believe that he is real and that he rewards those who truly want to find him.", Hebrews C11V6.

By any means necessary, it's time the Colored Males put an end to the blood bath and start promoting love, justice and good intentions in our communities and neighborhoods and it would make peace and justice more achievable. The Colored Male cannot afford to let fatigue or silence to continue to be blamed as the reason why Satan the Devil and disrespect continue to win the battle between evil over good. The spirit of love, justice and good intentions must give the Colored Male the confidence to help in the victory of "Good will conquer evil and Love will triumph over hate.

 Many Colored Males want to continue on the same path of greed, hate, and selfishness that led the world into an economical crisis. Money, sex, and drugs continue to be the number one obstacles to progress or change in our communities and neighborhoods Satan's cup of evil runneth over with blood from the Colored Male who continues to live and die by his wind pie and air sauce mentality. Colored Males must never forget where the spirit of peace and justice is there is freedom.

PROMOTE JUSTICE AND PEACE, NOT THE BLOOD BATH!

COLORED MALES V
By
Dave R. Queeley

VINCE DAVID **R.I.P.**

Too many has died in vain, no more dead bodies, caskets or grave sites. The record setting murder rate year of 2009 should have been a wakeup call to all Colored Males that life is short. Today all the unnecessary killings and shootings continue to happen for lack of knowledge about the Creators original plan of love, justice, and good intentions. In the 21st century too many Colored Males have relocated to the cemetery or life in prison AKA the modern day concentration camp that means Satan's angels of destruction continue to kill two birds with one stone.

Mr. Realistic AKA CNN of Love will teach the Colored Males about friendly fire that is more dangerous than enemy fire because they can see the enemy coming at them, but friendly fire comes from the people right there living with them in their communities and neighborhoods who they don't see as the enemy that's why it's so fatal and deadly to the Colored Males lives. They continue to be slaughtered and thrown into the streets like a piece of meat or garbage. No one is working to stop the massacre from happening.

The angel named Lucifer AKA Satan the Devil continues to use the Colored Males as disposable pawns in his attempt to conquer the world with disrespect. Colored Males must always remember there is an evil conspiracy to banish all traces of their past glory days of being servers of love, justice and good intentions. Disrespectful actions continue to play into the plans of the enemy to wipe out the Colored Males from society as grandfathers, brothers, or fathers. That's why the spiritual and mental genocide continues to decimate our communities and neighborhoods because too many Colored Males continue to walk around not knowing about the battle or the

Creators original plan of "Good will conquer evil and love will triumph over hate." Serving love, justice and good intentions can cure the lawlessness and disrespect that now plagues our communities and neighborhoods. The problem seemed too big for our government officials and law enforcement officers to solve and our communities and neighborhoods keep being close-minded to help making a difference.

With the murder rate once again on the rise in 2010 the problem seems staggering and those who struggle to confront it feels over matched by disrespect. Our communities and neighborhoods has gotten angrier and angrier over the last couple of years or decades and the spirit of love, justice and good intentions have completely switched sides to Satan, sinful ways, evil and disrespect which are the main problem that leads to all the killing and shootings. It's time for the Colored Males to accelerate the journey or mission back to the Creators original plans of "Good will conquer evil and love will triumph over hate." It appears as if they have taken a vacation from reality or respect because they continue to do all they can to invite further disaster upon their communities and neighborhoods by continue living for or dying for evil, sinful ways or disrespect. In the 21st century Colored Males need to learn the ethics and morals of serving love, justice and good intentions if they want to survive another five centuries.

Automatic gunfire continues to ring out at nighttime and no one calls the police. Two Colored Males get into a fight or argument, it turns ugly, someone gets shot and dies and believers just close their windows or blinds like nothing happened. All believers must remember guns and drugs are coming in on commercial or private aircrafts, cargo vessels, ships, yachts, and through the mail and they are pouring into our communities and neighborhoods at an alarming rate and falling into the wrong hands and no one knows where they came from or who are selling them. NOT GETTING INVOLVED should never be a part of true believers vocabulary. It's their fathers, uncles, and brothers who are dying. They should always GET INVOLVED because it's their communities and neighborhoods that continue to suffer from all these violent crimes.

Disrespect continues invading or conquering our communities and neighborhoods. True believers continue fighting about INVOLVMENT vs. NON-INVOLVMENT while disrespect continues to be making conquests in leaps and bounds. Violent crime has spiraled so far out of control that parental and military assistance needs to be called in to help fight this battle. Any murder of a Colored Male is a tragedy, the recent surge in violence is proof that NON-INVOLVMENT will not win the battle or war. Time to ring the alarm by any means necessary and let respect shine bright.

"GET INVOLVED AND SAVE A LIFE"

COLORED MALES   VI
THE LAST ONE
By
Dave R. Queeley

GROWTH AND DEVELOPMENT OR NOTHING

Live life to the fullest like it's the last days on Earth. It's time for a genuine approach to ending disrespect and violent behavior's reign as the King of the Hill.

COLORED MALES continue to live life like it's a video game where they can press restart when the game is over. Reality has not set in yet that with death. There is no restart. In the 21st century disrespect and violent behavior is a plague without a cure because life does not mean a thing anymore. A penny is worth more than life in the 21st century. All COLORED MALES must understand that respect is the Holy Grail to the spiritual and mental freedom and they must remember or realize no one is forced to serve evil, sinful ways and disrespect, they choose to, whether by force or by circumstance.

Disrespect and violent behavior continue waging war and creating havoc in their lives and there comes a time when they must learn to be respectful to human life because disrespect and violent behavior is the incarnation of all things evil and it continues to haunt COLORED MALES like ghosts in a haunted house, like every day is HALLOWEEN.

COLORED MALES must remember before they can respect anyone in their communities and neighborhoods they've got to START RESPECTING THEMSELVES FIRST and secondly, to return to the Creator's original plan of "Good will conquer evil and Love will triumph over hate." It's time COLORED MALES be proud to be a people of respect, honor and consciousness because Satan's sinful ways and disrespect continue to flip them like a fast food burger, it's a category 5 pain in the neck for our communities and neighborhoods. The crisis facing the COLORED MALE is deeply complicated by the fact that getting money or material possessions is their number one priority, not serving love, justice and good intentions.

They must remember serving love, justice, and good intentions is pivotal in the struggle to save the growing number of COLORED MALES that continue to relocate to the cemetery or life in prison. All believers must rejoice at the COLORED MALE who lives and survives to see the age of 30. Because every day on the radio or in the newspaper they read or hear about another tragedy or another violent stain on their history as the Creator's first people of Creation.

Our communities and neighborhoods must realize in the 21st century Satan the Devil AKA Lucifer continue to release his weapon of mass disrespect that continues to act as his I.E.D.'s and when they are tripped, another COLORED MALE lose their life.

No more record setting years for murders, because enough have died already. (45-2007:41-2008; 51-2009; 36 and counting-2010) Remember its GROWTH AND DEVELOPMENT OR NOTHING.

And it's as REAL AS IT GETS!